ISAAC ASIMOV'S NEW LIBRARY OF THE UNIVERSE

UFOs:
TRUE MYSTERIES OR HOAXES?

BY ISAAC ASIMOV
WITH REVISIONS AND UPDATING BY GREG WALZ-CHOJNACKI

Gareth Stevens Publishing
MILWAUKEE

For a free color catalog describing Gareth Stevens' list of high-quality books, call 1-800-542-2595 (USA) or 1-800-461-9120 (Canada). Gareth Stevens' Fax: (414) 225-0377.

Library of Congress Cataloging-in-Publication Data

Asimov, Isaac.
  UFOs : true mysteries or hoaxes? / by Isaac Asimov ; with revisions and updating by
Greg Walz-Chojnacki.
      p. cm. — (Isaac Asimov's new library of the universe)
  Rev. ed. of: Unidentified flying objects. 1988.
  Includes bibliographical references and index.
  ISBN 0-8368-1198-4
  1. Unidentified flying objects--Juvenile literature.
  I. Walz-Chojnacki, Greg, 1954-. II. Asimov, Isaac. Unidentified Flying Objects.
  III. Title. IV. Series: Asimov, Isaac. New library of the universe.
  TL789.2.A83   1995
  001.9'42—dc20   94-34043

This edition first published in 1995 by
Gareth Stevens Publishing
1555 North RiverCenter Drive, Suite 201
Milwaukee, Wisconsin 53212, USA

Project editor: Barbara J. Behm
Design adaptation: Helene Feider
Editorial assistant: Diane Laska
Production director: Susan Ashley
Picture research: Kathy Keller
Artwork commissioning: Kathy Keller and Laurie Shock

Printed in the United States of America

1 2 3 4 5 6 7 8 9 99 98 97 96 95

To bring this classic of young people's information up to date, the editors at Gareth Stevens Publishing have selected two noted science authors, Greg Walz-Chojnacki and Francis Reddy. Walz-Chojnacki and Reddy coauthored the recent book *Celestial Delights: The Best Astronomical Events Through 2001.*

Walz-Chojnacki is also the author of the book *Comet: The Story Behind Halley's Comet* and various articles about the space program. He was an editor of *Odyssey*, an astronomy and space technology magazine for young people, for eleven years.

Reddy is the author of nine books, including *Halley's Comet, Children's Atlas of the Universe, Children's Atlas of Earth Through Time,* and *Children's Atlas of Native Americans,* plus numerous articles. He was an editor of *Astronomy* magazine for several years.

CONTENTS

We live in an enormously large place – the Universe. It's just in the last fifty-five years or so that we've found out how large it probably is. It's only natural that we would want to understand the place in which we live, so scientists have developed instruments – such as radio telescopes, satellites, probes, and many more – that have told us far more about the Universe than could possibly be imagined.

We have seen planets up close. We have learned about quasars and pulsars, black holes, and supernovas. We have gathered amazing data about how the Universe may have come into being and how it may end. Nothing could be more astonishing.

But that doesn't mean we have solved everything about the Universe. Astronomers puzzle over objects they observe with their telescopes millions of light-years away. Other puzzling events occur very close to home. What are the strange lights in the sky people sometimes see without even using telescopes? These sightings are called unidentified flying objects, or UFOs. What can they possibly be?

Isaac Asimov

UFOs – Fact or Fancy?

Sometimes people see strange objects in the sky they can't explain. Because there doesn't seem to be a ready explanation for the objects, they are referred to as UFOs, or unidentified flying objects.

The present-day UFO excitement started in 1947, when pilot Kenneth Arnold saw a formation of bright circular objects skimming mountaintops. He described them as looking like saucers skipping across water. The term *flying saucers* caught on. But there have been other UFO sightings prior to this. Some go very far back in time, and not all of them were reported to look like saucers.

Left: Flying saucers – fact or fancy? Here's how one might appear in modern times.

Below: Pilot Kenneth Arnold saw UFOs from his plane one day in 1947.

UFOs in History

Hundreds, even thousands, of years ago, what did people think when they looked at the sky and saw things they could not explain? We do not know for certain.

However, vague stories and legends about UFOs have been told for centuries. In the 1500s, for instance, people reported seeing spheres and disks in the sky over Germany and Switzerland. According to the Bible, Elijah was carried up to heaven in a fiery chariot. Ezekiel reported seeing such a chariot.

? *Ezekiel's vision –*
UFOs in the Bible?

In the Bible, in the first chapter of the Book of Ezekiel, the prophet Ezekiel tells of a vision he had. He speaks about four humanlike creatures, but each with four faces and four wings, and each with hooves. What's more, the creatures were accompanied by wheels within wheels that moved with them. As the objects moved, there was a great noise. What did Ezekiel see? Should we conclude that the Book of Ezekiel reports a UFO sighting?

Opposite, top: An artist's depiction of Ezekiel's vision.

Opposite, bottom: According to reports, on August 7, 1566, a group of round objects appeared in the sky over Basel, Switzerland, and raced toward the Sun. Before vanishing, some of the objects turned toward each other, as if in combat.

UFOs Throughout the World

In 1896, people began reporting that they had seen cigar-shaped objects in the sky that looked like airships. A rash of such reports came from England and New Zealand between 1909 and 1913. Soon, similar reports poured in from many other countries.

? *The Great Pyramid – built by aliens?*

In about 2500 B.C., the ancient Egyptians built the Great Pyramid, which is made of about 2,300,000 blocks of stone, each weighing thousands of pounds. No one knows exactly how the Egyptians could have built such a mighty structure with their simple tools. Some people think that aliens from UFOs built the pyramid. But others wonder why such aliens would not have built the structure out of a more advanced material than stone.

Top: Strange disks and spheres reportedly followed United States aircraft on bombing missions over Europe during World War II. Sightings were reported on several occasions, and their origin remains a mystery to this day.

Bottom: In aerial photos taken near Nazca, Peru, lines reveal what look like runways for vehicles from other worlds. It is more likely, however, that the lines reveal roads built about A.D. 900 by people living in the area for use in special ceremonies.

Present-Day UFOs

People have been seeing brightly lit objects in the skies for ages. It is not difficult to imagine that UFOs may be advanced vehicles of some sort from worlds far away.

Some people have reported feeling heat, static electricity, sickness, or other odd sensations while they were in the area where the UFOs were sighted.

So what is true and what is imaginary? Unfortunately, it is hard to know what is really the truth from the various stories people relate.

Opposite: In the mid-1980s, several police officers saw an unusual object in the sky near Belleville, Wisconsin. Radar tracked the object, but no one has been able to explain what it was. This photo was taken in Belleville. The UFO has been added by an artist to give you an idea of what the people saw.

Below: Sometimes our imaginations make us think "flying saucer" when what we are really seeing is just a "flying object." What do the flying objects in these pictures taken in Hawaii *(left)* and Peru *(right)* look like to you?

Truth or Fiction?

There have been thousands of reports of UFO sightings, but nothing in the way of solid evidence. You would think that with all those ships flying through the air, at least one would have crashed or dropped some evidence to the ground! There have been photographs taken of UFOs, but they are not very clear or reliable.

Then, too, whenever a very sensational sighting is reported, there are suddenly dozens of other similar reports. Some UFO groups argue that these additional sightings confirm the first. They say a UFO announcement may encourage people to come forward with sightings they had been afraid to report earlier. But people often copycat, or imitate, each other and make false statements.

And none of these stories, so far, has produced any real evidence that says, "This came from a UFO!"

Left: Cradle Hill, in Warminster, Wiltshire, England, is the scene of several UFO sightings. Cradle Hill was known as a UFO "hot spot" in the 1960s.

Identified Flying Objects

There is no doubt that people sometimes see objects in the sky they don't understand. Many objects – meteor trails, the planet Venus, comets, odd-shaped clouds, ball lightning, burning marsh gases, airplanes, or the lights of distant cars – can seem mysterious, especially in the dead of night.

In addition, there may be lights in the sky for reasons that scientists do not yet understand or know how to explain.

Control tower to Venus: "You're cleared to land!"

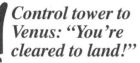

UFO investigator Allan Hendry told this story on a NOVA (Public Broadcasting System) episode entitled "The Case of the UFOs." Air traffic controllers in a busy airport were expecting the arrival of a flight in the eastern sky during dawn hours. When they spotted Venus out of the control tower window, they radioed the planet clearance to land! Hendry says this goes to show that "even the best-trained observers can be fooled by this unusually bright planet."

Top: On their way to becoming the first humans to land on the Moon, the *Apollo 11* astronauts spotted this strange object *(at right)* on July 16, 1969. Officials from the United States government have identified it as a piece of space "junk" from *Apollo*'s Saturn rocket. Others aren't so sure.

Center and bottom: Ball lightning and weather balloons are unfamiliar sights to most people.

Opposite, bottom: High-altitude, lens-shaped clouds can play tricks on the eyes, to make them seem like something they are not.

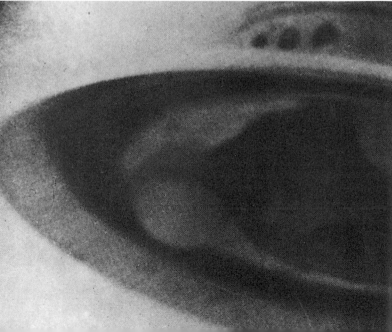

Is It a Bird? Is It a Plane?
No, It's a Fake.

Unfortunately, some people like to get their names in the papers, or have fun fooling people. It is easy to take a photograph of a spaceship model so it looks like it is floating in the sky. People can also create fake rows of lights. Sometimes, people make fake UFO pictures by just keeping the camera out of focus, or putting a drop of developer on a negative. Some hoaxers are quite skilled at making fake photographs of supposed UFOs.

Many of these hoaxes have been investigated and dismissed. The more hoaxes there are, the more difficult it is to believe *any* UFO reports.

! *Invasion from Mars!*

In 1938, actor/director Orson Welles broadcast a radio drama of H. G. Wells's The War of the Worlds. *In it, "news bulletins" stated that Martian ships were attacking New Jersey and then spreading over the United States. In the introduction to the radio play, Orson Welles had clearly said,* *"This is not truth. It is fiction." In addition, no astronomers at the time believed there was advanced life on Mars. But just the same, many people believed the story, and crowds of people in New Jersey got into their cars and fled in panic.*

Top: Would you be fooled by this fake UFO photo? Not if you saw the whole picture! To create this fake UFO, two paper-plate bowls were stapled together, highlights were added to the object with a felt-tip marker, and a "partner in crime" with the photographer threw the flying saucer.

Bottom: The man pictured with a telescope *(left)* is a UFO hoaxer. His flying saucer *(right)* is a fake.

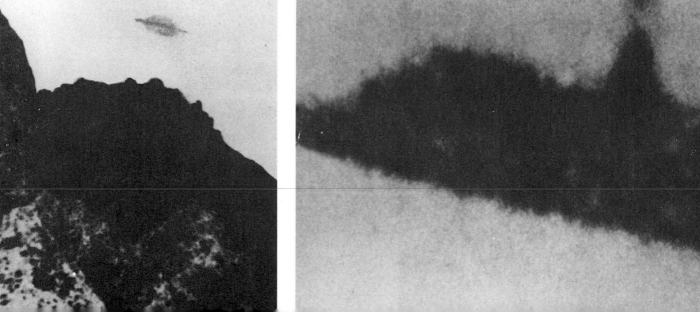

Earth Visitors

Perhaps the most popular definition of UFOs is that they are not only ships, but alien ships with beings from other worlds aboard them.

We understand enough about our Solar System today to know that if there are beings in outer space, they must live on worlds many light-years away. The trip from their world to our world would be difficult, requiring incredible amounts of energy, dedication, and sacrifice.

It is likely that our advanced instruments would detect an actual expedition approaching Earth from great distances. It is unlikely that so many different shapes and sizes of actual ships from other worlds would be able to buzz our planet for fifty years without being identified.

Opposite, top: One of the most famous "saucer" shots available was taken by Paul Trent in Oregon on the evening of May 11, 1950. The picture shows an object sailing over a toolshed in Trent's backyard. An enlarged detail of the same UFO is pictured at *bottom, right.* "It was very bright . . . and there was no noise or smoke," Mr. Trent said of the saucer. Added Mrs. Trent, "It was shiny but not as bright as a hubcap . . . and awfully pretty."

Top: This UFO was photographed in 1952 as it flew over a Brazilian coastal city.

Opposite, bottom, left: Taken by an official photographer of the Brazilian Navy on January 16, 1958, this photo has raised many questions. Even though the photographer was known for his trick photography, the Brazilian Navy has vouched for the accuracy of this photo.

What Do You Believe?

Many people think the government should investigate reports of UFO sightings with great care. After all, there is a possibility that UFOs just might be advanced aircraft developed by unfriendly nations for unfriendly purposes.

Government investigations almost always conclude that there is no proof of actual UFOs. The conclusions usually state that some sightings have natural explanations, some are hoaxes, and some are the result of panic or fear. Many people accept these conclusions. Others – such as the late J. Allen Hynek, an astronomer who once investigated UFO reports for the U.S. government – feel that government investigations are not as thorough or honest as they might be. And still others – mainly people who believe UFOs are alien vehicles – simply refuse to accept such conclusions from the government. They think the government is lying and hiding evidence.

Still, there are thousands of reports of UFO sightings. Are all of them wrong? Currently, scientists feel there is no real proof that flying saucers from other worlds exist.

Above: UFO researcher J. Allen Hynek felt the U.S. government was not doing enough to investigate UFO sightings.

? *When is a UFO not an unidentified flying object?*

There are many sensational books about UFOs. One book, The Roswell Incident, *tells of a flying saucer crash just two weeks after pilot Kenneth Arnold made his sighting in 1947. A rancher in New Mexico had found debris that seemed to have come from a crashed saucer. But a closer look at the evidence and a check with the U.S. Air Force revealed the truth. The debris was from a crashed radar balloon.*

Above: A rancher in New Mexico heard a crash late one night during a storm. He found his land littered with debris the next morning. Many people thought the debris was from a flying saucer! This painting shows what the rancher may have imagined to be happening outside his window that stormy night.

Left: Mysterious circles were found in a cornfield at the Devil's Punchbowl, Cheesefoot Head, Hampshire, England. Could they have been created by extraterrestrials? Many crop circles, such as these, have been found to be hoaxes.

21

A Continuing Controversy

Many people believe that UFOs are alien spaceships. The excitement surrounding UFO sightings is sensational, and some people like hearing about sensational things.

For example, in 1835, the *New York Sun* reported that a new and powerful telescope had discovered living creatures on the Moon. In fact, the report was a clever hoax by writer Richard A. Locke. Scientists already believed the Moon had neither air nor water and could not support life. But thousands believed the hoax.

It seems that sensational reports about UFOs will continue through the ages, and so will the controversy!

❗ *The end of the world!*

In the early 1800s, an American preacher named William Miller studied the Bible and concluded that the world would come to an end in March 1844. Thousands of people sold all their things and waited on a hilltop to be taken to heaven. Nothing happened. Miller predicted a new date of October 1844. Again, nothing happened.

Opposite: Some "believers" think this fifteenth-century Italian painting contains a UFO.

Below: These lights in the sky over South Island, New Zealand, remain unexplained.

Other Planets

If there are UFOs, where are they from? That's a good question, since so far we have not discovered any other planets beyond our Solar System. However, evidence for such "extrasolar planets" gets stronger every day.

In 1993, astronomers found a pulsar with small objects – planets – in orbit around it. However, no life could exist on a planet that orbits a pulsar. This is because pulsars are created by supernovas that would destroy any chance of life. In 1994, astronomers using the Hubble Space Telescope found disks in orbit around young stars in the Orion Nebula. These disks are just like the ones our Sun's planets came from. Such disks are much easier to spot than actual planets, though, and we still haven't found another sun with a solar system like ours. But this important discovery seems to confirm the idea that planets often form with stars.

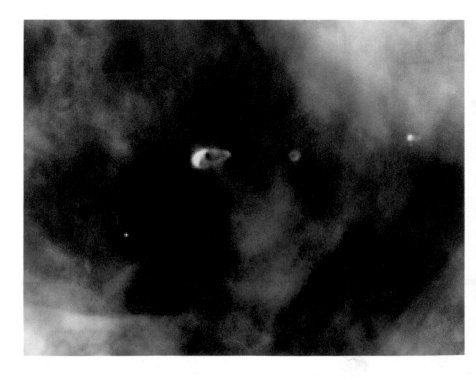

Right: A close-up of one of the proplyds, or disks, from the photo *above.* It contains at least 7 times the material as our Earth. It is 56 billion miles (90 billion kilometers) across or 7.5 times the size of our Solar System.

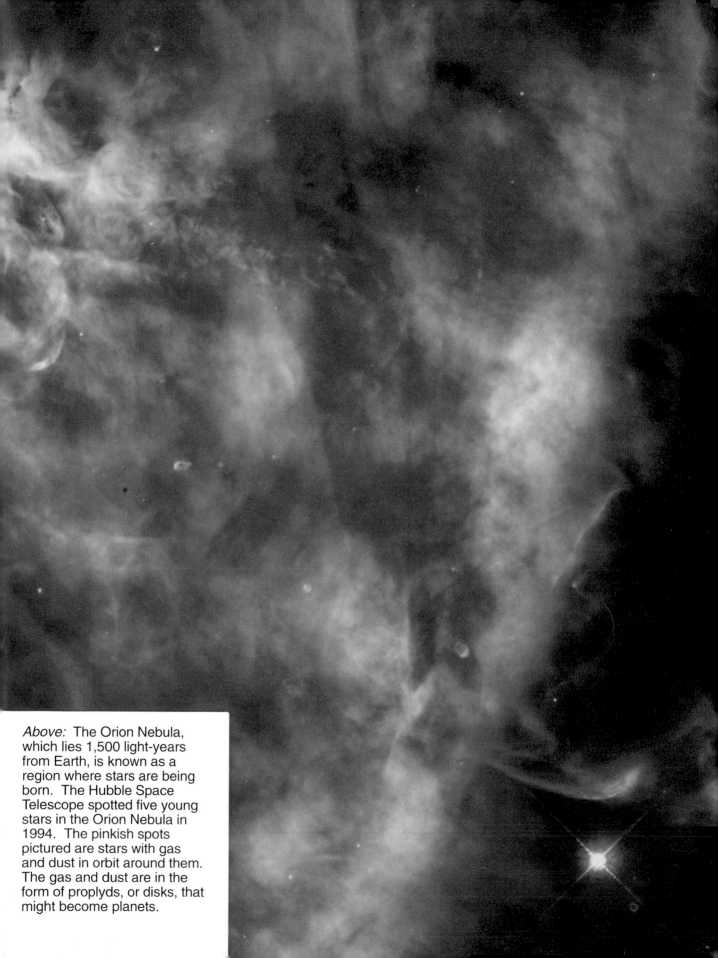

Above: The Orion Nebula, which lies 1,500 light-years from Earth, is known as a region where stars are being born. The Hubble Space Telescope spotted five young stars in the Orion Nebula in 1994. The pinkish spots pictured are stars with gas and dust in orbit around them. The gas and dust are in the form of proplyds, or disks, that might become planets.

Otherworldly

Is it possible there may be life on other worlds? Yes! After all, there are 200 billion stars in our Galaxy and at least 100 billion other galaxies. Among all those stars, a great many must be like the Sun and have planets like Earth.

J. Allen Hynek investigated 10,000 UFO sightings and concluded that about 500 could not be explained satisfactorily. By the time he died in 1986, however, he still had not been able to turn up any scientific evidence that would prove the existence of alien vehicles.

While most scientists are skeptical about UFOs, many believe alien life is possible – even likely. Large radio telescopes are used by scientists to listen for radio signals that could be signs of intelligent life on other worlds. Although no signals have yet been heard, many scientists believe it will not be long before careful searches detect other civilizations in the distant reaches of the Universe.

Left: An artist's conception of a family from another world enjoying an outing. Of the billions upon billions of stars in the Universe, couldn't at least a few million support planets with intelligent life?

Fact File: Distant and Close Encounters

People report encountering UFOs in many ways. J. Allen Hynek studied these ways and came up with two basic types of UFO encounters – distant sightings and close encounters.

In a distant sighting, a UFO appears too far away for anyone to determine what it might be or to describe it in detail. On the other hand, when people report a UFO at close range, it is called a close encounter. There are three kinds of close encounters, as defined by Hynek. These are referred to as close encounters of the first kind, second kind, and third kind.

1. Close Encounters of the First Kind – Sighting UFOs at Close Range

Most people who encounter UFOs only see them. In this kind of encounter, the UFO does not leave any physical evidence. Many people describe the UFO in detail, but even this kind of close encounter is rare.

Below: In this illustration of a close encounter of the first kind, a UFO hovers over a ship at sea. It is close enough to be sighted, reported, and even photographed by people on board the ship. But it has left no physical evidence. Many people doubt even photographic evidence of this kind of encounter.

What Should You Do If You Encounter a UFO?

• Don't panic.

• Remember that *UFO* means just that – unidentified flying object. *Unidentified* only means that you don't know what it is. Most objects people think of as UFOs really can be identified and explained.

• People often see bright stars, planets, comets, meteors, satellites, airplanes, and even birds – but think they see something else. Sometimes, unusual weather conditions make ordinary objects in the sky look unusual. So remember that a UFO is probably nothing to be frightened of. It's just something that you cannot identify – at least when you first see it.

• If you can, ask someone else – a parent, teacher, or other adult – to look at the UFO with you. Chances are they can tell you what it really is.

• Sometimes, newspapers and television and radio news programs can tell you what a UFO really was. When a satellite falls or when a meteor shower happens, it is news!

• If you have tried to find out about a UFO and still don't know what it is, ask an adult for more help. Sometimes, people at a museum or planetarium might be able to explain what a UFO you have seen really is.

3. Close Encounters of the Third Kind – Sighting or Contacting Beings In or Around UFOs

When people report seeing, contacting, or feeling the presence of beings in or near a UFO, Hynek determined they are reporting a close encounter of the third kind.

Top: This painting of a close encounter of the third kind illustrates one man's statement of having been taken by a saucerlike craft to a giant "mother ship" high above Earth. There, he claims to have met with handsome humanoids from Venus.

2. Close Encounters of the Second Kind – Physical Evidence or Effects from UFOs

Some people report that a UFO they have encountered leaves some kind of physical evidence, such as marks on the ground. Or they sometimes say that the presence of a UFO made them feel sick or that the UFO caused strange smells or sensations such as static electricity, strong magnetism, and heat.

Above: In this photograph of a possible close encounter of the second kind, authorities examine a presumed UFO landing site near Richmond, Virginia, in 1967. Most evidence of this sort is eventually found not to be from a flying saucer.

More Books about Unidentified Flying Objects

Aliens and Extraterrestrials – Are We Alone? Asimov (Gareth Stevens)
Creatures from UFOs. Cohen (Archway)
Monsters, Mysteries, UFOs. Spellman (Learning Works)
Nancy Drew: Flying Saucer Mystery. Keene (Wanderer Books)
UFO. Blumberg (Avon)
UFO Encounters. Gelman and Seligson (Scholastic)
A UFO Has Landed. Dank and Dank (Dell)

Video

Our Milky Way and Other Galaxies. (Gareth Stevens)

Places to Visit

Here are some museums and centers where you can find a variety of space exhibits.

The Space and Rocket Center
  and Space Camp
One Tranquility Base
Huntsville, AL 35807

Astrocentre
Royal Ontario Museum
100 Queen's Park
Toronto, Ontario M5S 2C6

National Air and Space Museum
Smithsonian Institution
Seventh and Independence Avenue SW
Washington, D.C. 20560

San Diego Aero-Space Museum
2001 Pan American Plaza
Balboa Park
San Diego, CA 92101

Anglo-Australian Observatory
Private Bag
Coonarbariban 2357 Australia

Seneca College Planetarium
1750 Finch Avenue East
North York, Ontario M2J 2X5

Places to Write

Here are some places you can write for more information about the study of the worlds beyond our Earth. Be sure to state what kind of information you would like. Include your full name and address so they can write back to you.

NASA Lewis Research Center
Educational Services Office
21000 Brookpark Road
Cleveland, OH 44135

Jet Propulsion Laboratory
Teacher Resource Center
4800 Oak Grove Drive
Pasadena, CA 91109

Canadian Space Agency
Communications Department
6767 Route de L'Aeroport
Saint Hubert, Quebec J3Y 8Y9

Sydney Observatory
P. O. Box K346
Haymarket 2000 Australia

Glossary

alien: in this book, a being from some place other than Earth.

ball lightning: an unusual form of lightning that is shaped like a ball.

billion: the number represented by 1 followed by nine zeroes – 1,000,000,000. In some countries, this number is called "a thousand million." In these countries, one billion would then be represented by 1 followed by twelve zeroes – 1,000,000,000,000 – a million million.

Close Encounters of the First Kind: UFO sightings at close range, according to a system developed by astronomer J. Allen Hynek. In this kind of sighting, other than the stories people tell of having seen them nearby, no actual physical evidence of an encounter with UFOs exists.

Close Encounters of the Second Kind: encounters with UFOs in which some kind of physical evidence or effects of a UFO exist.

Close Encounters of the Third Kind: encounters with UFOs in which people report seeing, physically contacting, or feeling the presence of beings in or near a UFO.

comet: an object made of ice, rock, and gas, with a tail that may be seen when the comet's orbit is close to the Sun.

developer: in this book, a chemical used to bring out the image on exposed photographic film. Developer can also be used to change an image to create misleading results.

galaxy: a large grouping of stars, gas, and dust that exists in the Universe. Our Galaxy is known as the Milky Way.

hoax: an act that is intended to deceive.

humanoid: resembling a human in appearance or having human features.

light-year: the distance traveled by light in one year – nearly 6 trillion miles (9.5 trillion km).

meteor: a meteoroid, or lump of rock or metal, that has entered Earth's atmosphere. Also, the bright streak of light made as the meteoroid enters or moves through the atmosphere.

negative: in this book, a piece of photographic film that is used to produce a photograph.

phenomena: remarkable occurrences or facts in the Universe.

pyramids: enormous structures built by the ancient Egyptians in about 2500 B.C. One pyramid may consist of as many as 2,300,000 blocks of stone.

skeptical: having doubts about statements that others generally feel are true.

UFO: the abbreviation for Unidentified Flying Object.

vehicles: machines that are used to transport people and materials.

Venus: a planet in our Solar System – the second planet from the Sun.

Index

Born in 1920, Isaac Asimov came to the United States as a young boy from his native Russia. As a young man, he was a student of biochemistry. In time, he became one of the most productive writers the world has ever known. His books cover a spectrum of topics, including science, history, language theory, fantasy, and science fiction. His brilliant imagination gained him the respect and admiration of adults and children alike. Sadly, Isaac Asimov died shortly after the publication of the first edition of *Isaac Asimov's Library of the Universe.*

The publishers wish to thank the following for permission to reproduce copyright material: front cover, © Julian Baum 1988; 4-5, © Mark Maxwell 1988; 5, 7 (upper), © David A. Hardy; 7 (lower), Courtesy of Julian Baum; 8, © Gary Milburn/Tom Stack and Associates; 8-9 (upper), © David A. Hardy; 8-9 (lower), © Gary Milburn/Tom Stack and Associates; 10 (both), Fortean Picture Library; 11, © Julian Baum 1988; 12-13, Fortean Picture Library; 14 (upper), © Julian Baum 1988; 14 (lower), National Severe Storms Laboratory; 14-15, NASA; 15, © Buff Corsi/Tom Stack and Associates; 16, Fortean Picture Library; 16-17 (upper), © Julian Baum 1988; 16-17 (lower), Courtesy of Julian Baum; 18-19 (all), Fortean Picture Library; 20, J. Allen Hynek Center for UFO Studies; 21 (upper), © David A. Hardy; 21 (lower), Fortean Picture Library; 22, 23, J. Allen Hynek Center for UFO Studies; 24, 25, C. R. O'Dell/Rice University/NASA; 26-27, © MariLynn Flynn 1988; 28, © Mark Dowman; 29 (upper), © David A. Hardy; 29 (lower), Fortean Picture Library.